CASE MEMORIAL LIBRARY, ORANGE

3 2159 00121 6338

W9-BTF-094

Withdrawn

BRAZIL

A TRUE BOOK

by
Ann Heinrichs

Children's Press®

A Division of Grolier Publishing

New York London Hong Kong Sydney
Danbury, Connecticut

CASE MEMORIAL
LIBRARY
ORANGE, CT 06477

Reading Consultant
Linda Cornwell
Learning Resource Consultant
Indiana Department of
Education

Dedicated to the memory
of Chico Mendes
(1944–1988)

A beach in Rio
de Janeiro

Library of Congress Cataloging-in-Publication Data

Heinrichs, Ann.
    Brazil / by Ann Heinrichs.
    p.   cm. — (A true book)
    Includes index.
    Summary: Introduces the history, geography, economy, people, and
culture of Brazil.
    ISBN 0-516-20328-2 (lib.bdg.)   0-516-26164-9 (pbk.)
    1. Brazil—Juvenile literature.   I. Title. II. Series.
F2508.5.H45   1997
981—dc20   96-28155
                                                    CIP
                                                    AC

© 1997 Children's Press®, a Division of Grolier Publishing Co., Inc.
All rights reserved. Published simultaneously in Canada.
Printed in the United States of America.
    5 6 7 8 9 10 R 06 05 04 03 02 01

Contents

A Diverse Land 5

People of Many Cultures 12

Colonial Times 18

From Empire to Republic 22

How People Live 25

Farms, Factories, and Mines 31

The Amazon Rain Forest 35

Festivals and Culture 40

To Find Out More 44

Important Words 46

Index 47

Meet the Author 48

ATLANTIC OCEAN

VENEZUELA

GUYANA
SURINAME
FRENCH
GUIANA

COLOMBIA

ECUADOR

Manaus

Amazon River

RAIN FOREST

BRAZIL

PERU

Brasília

BOLIVIA

Rio de
Janiero

N

PARAGUAY

Iguaçu
Falls

W   E

São Paulo

S

CHILE

ATLANTIC OCEAN

ARGENTINA

0   200 miles

URUGUAY

0   300 kilometers

PACIFIC OCEAN

BRAZIL

A Diverse Land

Brazil is the fifth-largest country in the world. It is also the largest nation in South America. On the north and east, the Atlantic Ocean washes up on Brazil's coast. Ten other South American countries border Brazil. The world's largest rain forest covers much of northern Brazil. There, chattering monkeys and colorful birds dart among the trees. Other rain forest animals include anteaters, caymans (alligator-like reptiles), and capybaras.

Winding through the rain forest is the mighty Amazon River. It is about 4,000 miles (6,437 kilometers) long. Thousands of rivers and streams flow into the Amazon. Only Egypt's Nile River is longer than the Amazon.

The Amazon River is the second-longest river in the world.

In the northeast, Brazil is dry and desertlike. Only the coastal strip in this region is good for farming.

Southern Brazil is a plateau of forests, grassland, and hills. Ranches and rich farmland thrive in the warm climate. The biggest cities in Brazil are found on the southern coast and plains.

In the southwest, Iguaçu Falls spills over steep cliffs into Argentina. This spectacular waterfall is more than 2 miles (3 kilometers) wide.

Rich soil for farming is found in southern Brazil (left). Visitors from all over the world marvel at the beauty of the Iguaçu Falls (below).

Capybaras

Capybaras are the largest rodents in the world. They grow up to 4 feet (1.2 meters) long and can weigh more than 100 pounds (45 kilograms)! Capybaras live along lakes and rivers.

They have reddish-brown or gray hair on their backs and yellowish-brown hair on their bellies. They have large heads and short tails. Their hind legs are longer than their front legs. Capybaras also have webbed toes, which make them excellent swimmers.

People of Many Cultures

More than 160 million people live in Brazil. About three of every five Brazilians are descended from Europeans, mainly Portuguese settlers. Others have German, Italian, African, or Spanish ancestors. Asian and Middle Eastern people also live in Brazil.

Brazil has more people than any other country in South America (above). Indians live in the Amazon region (right).

Indians lived in what is now Brazil long before the Europeans arrived. Today, they make up only about one percent of Brazil's population. Most of the Indians live in the Amazon region and in the far northern and western areas of the country. The Tupí-Guaraní is the largest Indian group.

Brazil is the only country in North or South America where Portuguese is the official language.

About three of four Brazilians live in the cities. Most large cities are near the Atlantic Coast, including São

Paulo, Brazil's biggest city, and Rio de Janeiro. Brasília is the nation's capital.

Portuguese (left) is a language similar to Spanish. Brazil's Congress meets in this building in Brasília (below).

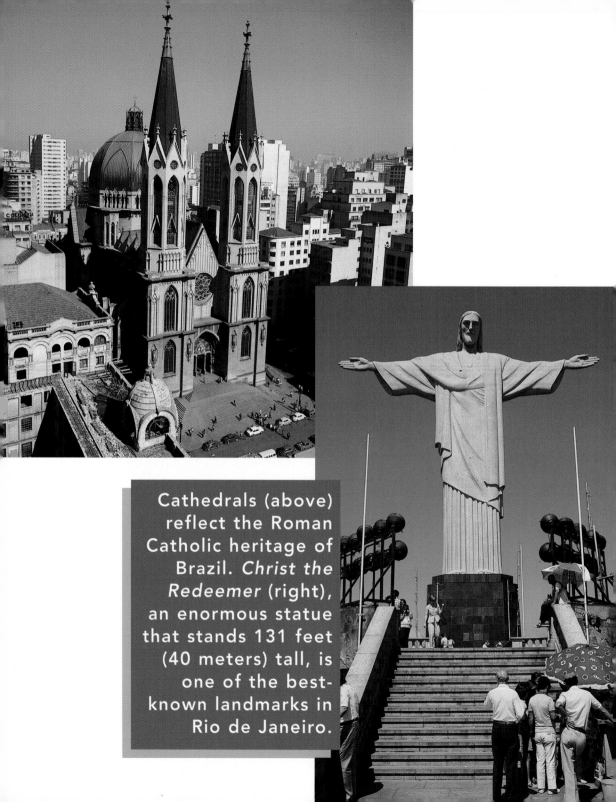

Cathedrals (above) reflect the Roman Catholic heritage of Brazil. *Christ the Redeemer* (right), an enormous statue that stands 131 feet (40 meters) tall, is one of the best-known landmarks in Rio de Janeiro.

Roman Catholicism is Brazil's major religion. More Catholics live in Brazil than in any other country in the world. Beautiful churches can be found throughout Brazil. Some of them are hundreds of years old. A world-famous statue called *Christ the Redeemer* sits atop Corcovado Mountain and overlooks Rio de Janeiro. The statue is 131 feet (40 meters) tall.

Colonial Times

Portugal's Pedro Álvares Cabral landed on the coast of what we now call Brazil in 1500 when his ship became lost in a storm. He claimed the region as a colony for Portugal.

Portuguese settlers began to arrive during the 1530s. They raised sugarcane on

Today, sugarcane is still raised on large plantations.

large plantations. Some settlers grew cotton and tobacco. The settlers often captured Indians for use as slaves. Many of the slaves died from diseases brought by the

Europeans. Many others were killed fighting the settlers. The Portuguese then brought thousands of slaves from Africa. Missionaries arrived from Portugal to bring the Roman Catholic religion to the Indians. Many of the missionaries also tried to protect the Indians from slavery.

Later, thousands of Portuguese rushed south to open mines when explorers found gold in 1698 and diamonds in 1729. Rio de Janeiro

Rio de Janeiro is a major port city in Brazil.

had an excellent harbor for shipping out these precious goods to other countries. It is still one of Brazil's busiest ports.

From Empire to Republic

In 1821, Emperor Pedro I declared Brazil's independence from Portugal. In 1889, Brazil became a republic with a constitution, a president, and a congress to make the laws. The official name of the country was the United States of Brazil. In 1967, the country's

Emperor Pedro I

name was changed to the Federative Republic of Brazil.

During the 1950s, Brazil's factories produced more goods than ever before. Cities grew, and many more products

CASE MEMORIAL
LIBRARY
ORANGE, CT 06477

Factories (above) employ thousands of Brazilians. Ships (right) carry products to other ports throughout the world.

were shipped to other countries. Today, however, Brazil faces some serious economic problems. But Brazil's leaders are working hard to make life better for all Brazilians.

How People Live

In Brazil, there are many rich people. There are also many poor people. Upper-class Brazilians drive expensive cars and live in beautiful homes. Most middle-class Brazilians live in rented apartments or houses. Many use buses or subway trains to travel.

Many upper-class Brazilians live in expensive homes (left). Most of Brazil's poor live in slums called *favelas* (below).

Millions of poor people live in big-city slums called *favelas*. Outside the cities, rural people live simply. Their homes are made of adobe, or sun-dried clay. The roofs are made of clay tile. Rural people use horses to travel.

In the Amazon region, Indians live in homes made of tree branches or plant stalks. They bind palm leaves together

Many people who live in rural areas use horses or donkeys to travel.

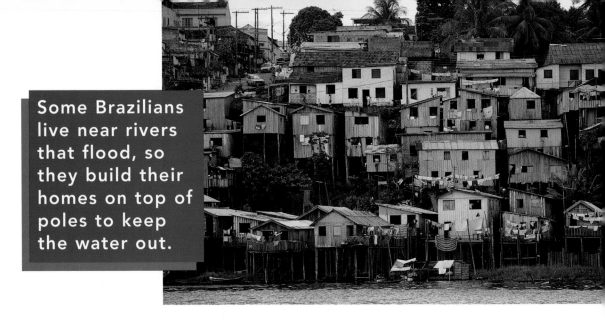

Some Brazilians live near rivers that flood, so they build their homes on top of poles to keep the water out.

to form a roof. People who live near rivers that flood build their homes on high poles.

Many more foods are available in the cities than in rural areas. But throughout the country, Brazilians enjoy eating *feijoada.* This is a delicious stew of black beans, dried beef, and pork. A

popular food in southern Brazil
is *churrasco*—beef roasted on a
stick. A favorite dish for people
who live in the northern region is
vatapá. It is made with shrimp
and fish cooked in coconut milk.

Churrasco is
very popular in
southern Brazil.

Brazilians love playing soccer.
They are especially proud of their
many soccer stars. Brazil won the
World Cup Championship in
1994. Maracanã Stadium in Rio
de Janeiro is the largest soccer
stadium in the world.

Farms, Factories, and Mines

Many valuable products grow on Brazil's farms and in the forests. Brazil is well known throughout the world for its delicious coffee. Brazil provides one-fourth of the world's coffee.

Sugarcane is also grown in Brazil. Besides its use as a

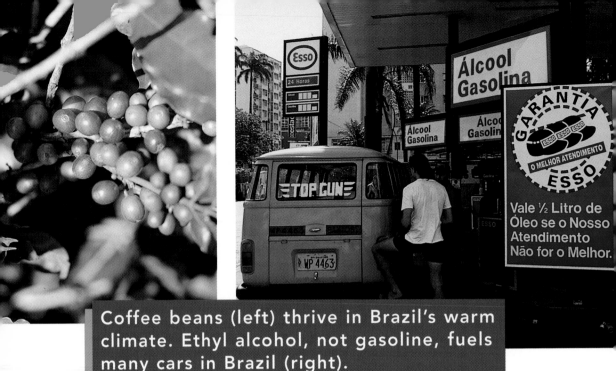

Coffee beans (left) thrive in Brazil's warm climate. Ethyl alcohol, not gasoline, fuels many cars in Brazil (right).

sweetener, it is also made into a fuel called ethyl alcohol. Most cars made in Brazil run on ethyl alcohol instead of gasoline. Ethyl alcohol is cheaper than gasoline, and it keeps the air cleaner.

Oranges, bananas, and nuts are other important products in Brazil. In forests, araucaria trees are cut for lumber. Rubber trees ooze latex, which is collected for use in factories to make rubber. Most of Brazil's factories are in the southern region of the country. There, steel, cars, and other products are also made.

Many of Brazil's riches lie underground. Brazil has the world's largest supply of iron.

Latex oozes from a rubber tree (left). This gold mine (right) is 984 feet (300 meters) deep.

Quartz crystals, gem stones, gold, and dozens of minerals also come from the country's mines.

The Amazon Rain Forest

In the Amazon rain forest, Indians continue to live as their ancestors did. They hunt with spears and blowguns. They fish with hooks or spears in canoes carved from tree trunks.

From their ancestors, Brazil's Indians learned that certain plants and insects can

Many rain forest Indians fish from dugout canoes (above). Amazonian Indians use blowguns to hunt animals (right).

heal injuries or cure diseases. Today, many scientists study the medicinal plants found in the rain forest.

Unfortunately, some of Brazil's rain forest has been destroyed by logging and mining companies. Brazilians—and many people around the world—are trying to save the rain forest and its animals.

This section of Brazilian rain forest has been completely cut down.

The Amazon River

The Amazon River has many tributaries, or smaller rivers that flow into it. One of the Amazon's largest tributaries is the Negro River. Its waters are dark brown. The Amazon is light brown before the Negro joins it.

Negro River

Manaus

Amazon River

BRAZIL

Brasília

When the two rivers meet, their colors mix and swirl together. You can visit the place where the colors of the rivers meet. It is near the city of Manaus, about 1,200 miles (1,931 kilometers) northwest of the capital of Brasília.

Festivals and Culture

Brazil's biggest festival is called Carnaval. It is held in Rio de Janeiro. It takes place in the spring, just before the Christian holy season of Lent. Thousands of people enjoy the parades, the dazzling costumes, and the colorful dancers.

The festival of Carnaval attracts thousands of people to Brazil each year.

Brazilian music is popular all over the world. Brazilian jazz musicians include Antonio Carlos Jobim and João Gilberto. Heitor Villa-Lobos was a famous composer.

Fine art museums can be found in São Paulo and Rio de Janeiro. Brazilian artists include Cândido Portinari, known for his huge murals, or wall paintings.

Brazil is a country of great diversity and rich history.

Brazilians truly have a rich culture and have made many important contributions to the world.

To Find Out More

Here are some additional resources to help you learn more about the nation of Brazil:

 **Books**

 **Organizations**

Bailey, Donna and Anna Sproule. **Brazil.** Raintree Steck-Vaughn, 1990.

Cobb, Vicki. **This Place Is Wet.** Walker & Co., 1989.

Lewington, Anna. **What Do We Know About: The Amazonian Indians?** Peter Bedrick Books, 1993.

Morrison, Marion. **Brazil.** Raintree Steck-Vaughn, 1993.

Organization of American States (OAS)
17th Street & Constitution Avenue, NW Washington, DC 20006

Rainforest Action Network
450 Sansome Street
Suite 700
San Francisco, CA 94111
e-mail: *ran-info@ran.org*

United Nations Information Centre
1775 K Street, NW
Washington, DC 20008

Online Sites

Brazilian Mall
http://www.deltanet.com/ brazil/index.htm

Here you'll find information and photos on Brazil's beaches, natives, sports, music, culture, food, and more. Written in both English and Portuguese, you can learn some Portuguese words while you browse!

Brazil Photo Library
http://prairienet.org/ ~magiger/br_photo.html

Beautiful color photos of Iguaçu Falls, Rio de Janeiro, and many other places in Brazil

Kids World 2000: Museums Around the World
http://www.clever.net/ NOW/bigkidnetwork/ museums.html

Includes a visit to the Museu Paulista da USP-Ipiranga in Brazil

Important Words

ancestors relatives who lived long ago

colony territory owned by another country

plantation a large farm, usually with just one crop

plateau a large area of land that is much higher than the land on either side

rain forest forest with heavy rainfall and tall, broad-leaved trees

republic government that is ruled by a president instead of a king or queen

rodent a furry animal with two large, sharp front teeth

Index

(**Boldface** page numbers indicate illustrations.)

Africa, 20
Amazon River, 6, **7**, 38–39, **38**, **39**
araucaria trees, 33
Argentina, 8
Atlantic Ocean, 5
Brasília, 15, 39
capybaras, 6, 10–11, **10**, **11**
Carnaval, 40, **41**
Christ the Redeemer, **16**, 17
churrasco, 29, **29**
coffee, 31
Corcovado Mountain, 17
Emperor Pedro I, 22, **23**
ethyl alcohol, 32
Europeans, 12, 13, 20
factories, 23, **24**, 33
favelas, 26, **26**
Federative Republic of Brazil, 23
feijoada, 28
Iguaçu Falls, 8, **9**

Indians, 13–14, **13**, 19–20, 27-28, 35, **36**
iron, 33
Manaus, 39
Maracanã Stadium, 30, **30**
Negro River. *See* Amazon River
Pedro Álvares Cabral, 18
plantations, 19
plateau, 8
Portugal, 18, 20, 22
Portuguese, 14, **15**
rain forest, 5–6, 35–37, **37**
Rio de Janeiro, 15, 17, 20–21, **21**, 30, 40, 42
Roman Catholicism, 17, 20
rubber trees, 33, **34**
São Paulo, 14–15, 42
South America, 5, 14
sugarcane, 31
Tupí-Guaraní. *See* Indians
United States of Brazil, 22
vatapá, 29

Meet the Author

Ann Heinrichs grew up in Arkansas and lives in Chicago, Illinois. She has written more than twenty books about American, Asian, and African history and culture. She has also written numerous newspaper, magazine, and encyclopedia articles.

Besides the United States, she has traveled in Europe, North Africa, the Middle East, and east Asia. The desert is her favorite terrain.

Ms. Heinrichs holds bachelor's and master's degrees in piano performance. For relaxation, she practices chi gung and t'ai chi.

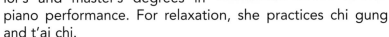

Photo Credits ©: Buddy Mays/Travel Stock:1, 13 bottom, 24 right, 38; Cameramann International, Ltd: cover, 13 top, 15 inset, 19; Chip and Rosa Maria Peterson: 24 left, 26 right, 32 left, 34 right; Robert Fried: 9 bottom, 29, 34 left, 39 both photos, 43; Robert Holmes: 2, 21; South American Pictures: 7 (Peter Dixon), 27, 28, 32 right, 37, 41 (Tony Morrison), 36 left (Bill Leimbach), 23, (Courtesy of South American Pictures); SuperStock: 9 top, 10, 11 both photos, 15 bottom, 16 both photos, 26 left, 30, 36 right

CASE MEMORIAL
LIBRARY
ORANGE, CT 06477